Short Treatise on
Political Power

Short Treatise on Political Power

ABRIDGED AND
ANNOTATED

John Ponet

Anthony Comegna, Editor

LIBERTARIANISM.ORG
WASHINGTON, DC

CONTENTS

From Where Political Power Grows

In his 1787 *Defence of the Constitutions of Government of the United States of America*, John Adams reflected that "there have been three periods in the history of England, in which the principles of government have been anxiously studied, and very valuable productions published." Although many of these venerable tomes were by then "wholly forgotten in their native country," the best of them "are perhaps more frequently read abroad." Included among these great political treatises, Adams asserted, was John Ponet's *Short Treatise on Political Power* (1556). Published while Ponet was in exile and "Bloody" Mary briefly restored Catholic rule to England, Ponet's decidedly *Protestant* political tract "contains all the essential principles of liberty," rediscovered during the Interregnum period (ca. 1640-1660). Adams wrote that in the seventeenth and eighteenth centuries, "Sidney, Locke, Hoadley, Trenchard, Gordon, Plato Redivivus," and others revived Ponet's ideas. Post-Revolutionary War Americans, John Adams argued, "should make collections of all these speculations, to be preserved as the most precious relics of antiquity both for curiosity and use." On John Adams's always-sincere advice, therefore, we have republished (abridged, with short annotations) this powerful and early exposition of revolutionary liberalism. In the first chapter, Ponet establishes the source, purpose, and limits of political power. In the next selection, we will examine the political and religious context in which he wrote and Ponet's argument that even monarchs are subject to the rule of law.

Chapter I. From Where Political Power Grows, for what purpose it was ordained, and the right use and duties of the same: & etc.

As oxen, sheep, goats, and other such unreason-

able creatures cannot for lack of reason rule themselves, but must be ruled by a more excellent creature, that is man: so man, although he has reason,
yet because through the fall of the first man, his reason is radically corrupt, and sensuality has gotten the
upper hand, he is not able by himself to rule himself,
but must have a more excellent governor. Those of
this world thought that this governor was their own
reason. They thought that they by their own reason might do the things they lusted for, not only
in private matters, but also in public. They thought
reason to be the only cause that men first assembled
themselves together in companies, that commonwealths were designed, that policies were well governed and long continued: but those of that mind
were utterly blinded and deceived in their imaginations, their works and inventions (though they
never seemed so wise) were so easily and so soon
(contrary to their expectations) overthrown.

Where is the wisdom of the Greeks? Where is the
fortitude of the Iberians? Where is both the wisdom
and the force of the Romans gone? All have van-
ished away, nothing almost left to testify that they
were, but that which declares well, that their reason
was not able to govern them. Therefore, such were
desirous to know the perfect and the only governor of all, constrained to seek further than themselves, and so at length to confess, that it was one
God that ruled all. By Him we live, we move, and
we have our being. He made us, and not we our-

selves. We are His people, and the sheep of His pasture. He made all things for man: and man He made for Himself, to serve and Glorify Him. He has taken upon Himself the order and government of man, His chief creature, and prescribed a rule to him, how he should behave himself, what he should do, and what he may not do.

This rule is the law of nature, first planted and grafted only in the mind of man, then after that his mind was defiled by sin, filled with darkness, and encumbered with many doubts. God set this rule forth in writing in the Decalogue, or the Ten Commandments: and after that, reduced by Christ our Savior to just two commands: You will love the Lord your God above all things, and your neighbor as yourself. The latter part He also expounded on: Whatever you would want done unto yourself, do that unto others.

In this law is compiled all justice, the perfect way to serve and glorify God, and the right means to rule each and every man: and the only stay to maintain every commonwealth. This is the touchstone to try every man's works, whether he is king or beggar, whether he be good or evil. By this all men's laws will be discerned, whether they be just or unjust, godly or wicked. For example; those that have authority to make laws in a commonwealth, make this law, that no punishment be imposed, but in their own country. This seems to be a trifling matter. Yet if by this means the people may be kept from idleness, it is a good and just law and pleases God. For idleness is a vice by which God is offended: and the way to offend Him in breach of the commandments: you shall not steal, you shall not kill, you shall not commit adultery, etc. For all these evils come from idleness. On the other side, if the people are well occupied in other things, and the people of another country live by pin making, and uttering them: if there should be a law made, that they may not sell them to their neighboring country, which is otherwise well occupied, it is a wicked and an unjust law. For taking away the means, whereby they live, a course is devised to kill them with famine, and so not only is this commandment broken, you shall not kill, but also the general law, which says: You shall love your neighbor as yourself; And, whatever you would want done unto yourself, do that unto others, for you yourselves would not be killed with hunger.

Likewise, if there is a law made, utterly prohibiting that any man can remain chaste, and cannot marry, this is an unjust, an ungodly, and a wicked law. For it is an occasion, that with marriage, he might avoid sinning: But if he does not marry, he commits fornication and adultery in act or thought contrary to God's will and commandment; You shall not commit adultery.

Again, a prince forces his subjects (under the name of request) to lend him what they have, which they do unwillingly: and yet for fear of a worse turn, they must seem to be content with the action. Afterwards, he causes a Parliament to be assembled as if he had been lent nothing at all, and they dare not displease him. To please him, they remit this general debt. This is a wicked and an unjust law. For they are not acting as they would want acted upon, but be an occasion, that a great number of people are undone, their children perish by famine for lack of sustenance, and their servants are forced to steal, and even possibly commit murder. So if men will weigh this order and law that God has proscribed to man–thou shalt love the Lord God above all things, and your neighbor as yourself. And, what ever you will have men do to you, do the same to them: they may soon learn to discern good from evil, godliness from ungodliness, right from wrong.

And it is so plain and easy to be understood, that any plea of ignorance can or will excuse him that causes offense in this manner....

By [the Ten Commandments] He instituted political power and gave authority to men to make more laws. For He that gave man authority over the body and life of man, because He would have man to live quietly with man, that all might serve Him quietly in holiness and righteousness all the days of his life, it cannot be denied, but He gave him authority over goods, lands, possessions, and all such things that may breed controversy and discord, and so hinder the service and worship that

He requires....But whether this authority to make laws, or the power to execute the same, shall be and remain in one person alone, or in many, it is not expressed, but left to the discretion of the people to make so many and so few, as the think necessary for the maintenance of the state....

And these diverse kinds of states or policies have distinct names, as where one ruled, a Monarchy: where many of the best, Aristocracy: where the multitude, Democracy: and where all together, that is, a king, the nobility, and commoners, a mixed state: which men by long continuance have judged to be the best sort of all. For where that mixed state was exercised, there did the commonwealth longest continue. But yet every kind of these states tended to one end, that is, to the maintenance of justice, to the wealth and benefit of the whole multitude, and not of the superior and governors alone. And when they saw that the governors abused their authority, they altered the state....The rich would oppress the poor, and the poor seek the destruction of the rich, to have what the rich had: the mighty would destroy the weak, and as Theodoretus says, "the great fish eats up the small", and the weak seeks revenge on the mighty: and so one seeking the other's destruction, all at length should be undone and come to destruction...

And the wonderful providence of God is herein to be well noted and considered, of all such as love and fear God, that in all places and counties where

God's word has been received and embraced, there for the time the people followed God, no tyranny could enter, but all the members of the body sought the prosperity and wealth of one another, for God's word taught them to do this. You shall love the Lord your God (it says) above all things, and your neighbor as yourself. And, what you will have men do unto you, do you also to them. The fruit of His word is love one another, whatever state or degree in this world they be in. And the state of the policies and commonwealths have been disposed and ordained by God, that the heads could not (if they would) oppress the other members....

If he ought to be sharply used, who deceives one poor man, how much more sharply ought he to be punished, and of all men to be abhorred (yes, and even cast unto the dogs) that deceives the whole of the realm of ten or twenty hundred thousand persons? If he is thus to be punished and abhorred who is required to do another man's business, and deceives him, how much more ought they to be abhorred and hated, that takes upon them to do for others, not desired but sung for it: not called thereto, but trusting in themselves: not praying, but paying, giving many liveries, procuring and making friends to give them their voice, obtaining great men's letters, and ladies' tokens, feasting freeholders, and making great bankletting cheer: not by the consent of the party, but by force and strength, with troops of horsemen, bills, bows, pikes, guns, and such of like kind and quality.

If this opinion be held, and judgment given against a man that seeks his own gain with the loss of his friends in small things: what opinions men have, what judgment shall be given of those that, intending to make themselves noble and rich, cuts the throats of those that committed themselves, their wives, their children, their goods, yes, and even their lives upon trust in to their hands?

If this judgment is given for worldly things, what judgment shall be given to those that willfully go about to destroy men's souls, and to make them a present to the devil, so that they for a time may be his deputies here on earth? If men abhor and punish such that are unfaithful and dishonest persons, how much more will the Almighty God abhor, condemn, and exercise His severe judgment upon them that abuse the authority given to them by Him, and deceive and undo those poor sheep of His, in whom (as His ministers) they put their trust?

Listen, listen (while there is time for repentance) to the sentence of God, pronounced by the mouth of his servant Isaiah; "Wo be unto you that make unrighteous laws, and devise things which are hard to be kept, whereby the poor are oppressed on every side, and the innocent of my people are robbed of judgment, that widows may be your prey, and that you may rob the fatherless. What will you do in the time of the visitation and destruction that shall come from afar? To whom will you run to for help? Or to whom will you give your honor, that he may keep you from becoming prisoners, or lie among the dead?

This terrible woe of everlasting damnation was spoken not only to Jerusalem, but to Germany, Italy, France, Spain, England, Scotland, and all other countries and nations, where the like vices shall be committed. For God is just, and hates sin, that He never leaves it in any place unpunished: but the more common it is, the greater plagues and force does He use to repress it: as we may learn from the examples of the cities of Sodom and Gomorrah, and Jerusalem, His own city. And besides the general plague, he whips the authors of it with some special scourge, that they may be a spectacle, not only to those that are present, but also a remembrance to all that are to come.

But some, who are put in trust and authority to make the laws and statutes, will say that they would not do anything willingly against God's honor, or the wealth of our country, or deceive any that put their trust in us.

If any such thing follows, it is by reason that we were ignorant....

Do you think that this bald excuse will serve? Is it not written, that if the blind leads the blind, both shall fall into the pit? Did the plea that Eve made for offending in eating the forbidden fruit (when she said that the serpent had deceived her) excuse her? Nothing less. She was not only herself punished with pains (none greater than death could be devised) but also all her posterity.

Perhaps others of you will say that you do not dare to do otherwise. If you did, you should be taken for enemies of the governor, running into indignation, and so lose your bodies and goods, and undo your children. O you that are faint of heart, do you think that your parents would have left you as you were found, if they were so faint of heart? Or do you think that you will serve your turn? Was it enough for Adam, our first father, when he fell with his wife in eating the forbidden fruit, to say, "I dare not displease my wife." Or to say as he said, "The woman that you gave me, gave the fruit to me?" No, it did not avail, but he and all his posterity were plagued for his disobedience, as we and all that shall follow us will do, if we have any fear of God before our eyes....

Thus you have heard not only from where political power grows, and of the true use and duty thereof, but also what will be laid to their charge, those that do not do their duty in making laws. Now see, what is said by God to the executors of the laws: "See what you do, for you execute not the judgment of man, but of God. And whatever you judge, it shall be rebounded to yourselves." Let the fear of God be before your eyes, and do all things with diligence. For with the Lord our God there is no iniquity, neither difference among persons, nor does He have pleasure in rewards or bribes.

But of the ministers of the laws and governors of realms and countries, more shall be said hereafter.

No King or Governor
Is Exempted

When Martin Luther nailed his ninety-five theses to
the door of the Wittenberg Cathedral in 1517, he inau-
gurated a movement that transformed European civilization. During the ensuing "Century of Iron" (ca.
1520s-1650s), Europeans slaughtered one another in
wholesale orgies of religious violence throughout the
entire continent: First were the German peasant rebel-
lions. Protestants seized Switzerland and fought
Catholic forces. Catholic armies under the Holy Roman
Emperor attempted to crush the Lutheran Schmalkaldic
League. Dutch Protestants revolted against the Catholic
Austrian *and* Spanish Hapsburgs for *eighty years*. As
many as *four million* French died as a result of their own

thirty-six years of religious civil war. *Eight million* Europeans (including roughly ten per cent of all Germans) expired during the Thirty Years War (1618-1648). The English Civil War remains the most costly war in British history (when the death toll is measured as a percentage of the population). Through it all—and the above list is *far* from exhaustive—the people suffered and states grew immensely powerful. Empire fueled war, war fueled empire, and by the end of the "Century of Iron," massive nation-state militaries and navies battled each other on a global scale for the first time in human history.

It was in this context of intense intellectual, political, and social upheaval that the Anglican Bishop of Winchester began his theological studies. John Ponet earned his BA from Queens' College, Cambridge in 1533 and his MA in 1535. From Queens', Ponet joined the Anglican priesthood, inaugurating a somewhat short, though fabulously storied, career in the church. Always the renegade, Ponet defied the Parliament's standing ban on clerical marriage and wed in 1548. He was arrested in 1549 for his involvement in court intrigue, but Ponet emerged from the affair being elected Bishop. Nevertheless, the Catholic reconquest of England during the reign of Mary I (1553-1558) claimed many victims, Ponet among them. Fleeing with roughly 800 fellow Protestant elites, Ponet spent the last years of his life exiled in Strasbourg. Seething, stuck in Germany, and fuming with hatred for the Catholic queen of

England, Ponet published his *Short Treatise on Political Power* shortly before his death (1556). In this second set of selections from Ponet, our very agitated author condemns the notion of absolute government authority and argues that *all men* are subject to the laws of nature.

Chapter II. Whether Kings, Princes, and other Governors have absolute power and authority over their subjects.

For as much as those that be the rulers in the world, and would be taken for gods (that is, the ministers and images of God here on earth, the examples and mirrors of all godliness, justice, equity, and other virtues) claim and exercise an absolute power, which also they call a fullness of power, or prerogative to do what they lust, and none may contradict them: to dispense with the laws as it pleases them, freely and without correction or offense do contrary to the law of nature, and other god's laws, and the positive laws and customs of their countries, or break them: and use their subjects as men do their animals, and as lords do their villains and bondsmen, getting their goods from them by hook and crook, with *sic volo, sic jubeo*, and spending it to the destruction of their subjects: the misery of this time requires us to examine whether they do it rightfully or wrongfully, that if it be rightful, the people may the more willingly obey and receive the same: if it be wrongful, then those that use it may leave it for fear of God. For (no doubt) God will come and judge the world with equity, and revenge the cause of the oppressed. Of the popes power (who believes himself one, yes, the chief of these kind of gods, yes, above them all, and fellow to the God of God's) we mind not now to treat: no other is a requisite. For all men, yes half women and babes can well judge, that his power is worthy to be laughed at: and were it not bolstered and propped up with the sword and faggot, it would (as it will notwithstanding) shortly lie in the mire, for it is not built on the Rock, but on sand, not planted by the Father of Heaven, but by the devil of hell, as the fruits manifestly declare. But we will speak of the power of kings and princes, and such potentates, rulers, and governors of commonwealths.

Before you have heard how for a great long time, that is until after the general flood, there was no civil or political power, and how it was then first ordained by God Himself, and for what purpose He ordained it: that is (to comprehend all briefly) to maintain justice: for everyone doing his duty to God, and one to another, is but justice. You have heard also how states, political bodies, and commonwealths have authority to make laws for the maintenance of the policy, so that they are not contrary to God's law and the laws of nature: which, if you note well the question before propounded whether kings and princes have absolute power, shall appear not doubtful, or if any world affirms it, that he shall not be able to maintain it. First with God's laws (by which name also the laws of nature are comprehended) kings and princes are not joined makers here with God, so that thereby of themselves they might claim any interest or authority to dissolve them or dispense with them, by this maxim or principal, that He that may knit together, may loose asunder: and He that may make, may marry: for before magistrates were, God's laws were. Neither can it be proved that by God's word they have any authority to dispense or break them: but that they are still commanded to do right, to minister justice, and not to swerve, neither on the right hand or on the left….

If we will not submit ourselves to God's judgment expressed by His word, as Christians should, let us mark the result: and thereby gather God's judgment, as Ethnarcs do. For when we have wrought our wits, and devised and done what we can, we can not exclude God, but He will have a word with us.

God's word, will and commandment is, that he that willfully kills a man, shall also be killed by man: that is, the magistrate. But this law has not

17

been observed and all ways executed, but kings and princes upon affection have dispensed and broken it, granting life and liberty to traitors, robbers, murderers, and etc.

But what has followed as a result of it? Have they (whose offenses have been so pardoned) afterwards shown themselves penitent to God, and thankfully profitable to the commonwealth? No, God and the commonwealth have had no greater enemies. They have added murder to murder, mischief to mischief, and of private malefactors, have become public, and of men killers, they have at length grown to be destroyers of their country, yes and many times those that have been saved from hanging and other just pains of the law. And this is no marvel: for God does not only punish the principals and authors of such mischief, but also those that are accessories and maintainers of it, and plagues iniquity with iniquity. You may likewise see what fruits have followed, were popes have dispensed, that marriages might be made contrary to God's laws. We shall not need to rehearse any? The end will declare all. But let us leave to reason that, wherein something may be said: that is, whether kings and princes may do things contrary to the positive laws of their country. For example:

It is a positive law that a mean kind of apparel, or a mean kind of diet should be used in a commonwealth, to the intent that men leaning the excess thereof, where many occasions both to destroy nature and to offend God follow, they might convert that they spent evil, to the relief of the poverty, or defense of their country.

Answer this question, this division ought to be made, that there be two kinds of kings, princes, and governors.

The one, who alone may make positive laws, because the whole state and body of their country have given, and resigned to them their authority to do so: which nevertheless is rather to be thought a tyranny than a king, as Dionisius, Philippus, and Alexander were, who saved whom they would and plundered whom they desired. And the other be such, unto whom the people have not given such authority, but keep it themselves: as we have before said concerning the mixed state.

It is true that in indifferent matters, that is of themselves be neither good nor evil, hurtful, or profitable, but for a decent order: kings and princes (to whom the people have given their authority) may make such laws, and dispense with them. But in matters that are not indifferent, but godly and profitably ordained for the commonwealth, they can not (for all their authority) break them or dispense with them....

If this were tolerable, then is it in vain to make solemn assemblies of the whole state and long parliaments? Yes (I beseech you) what certainty should there be in anything, where all should depend on one's will and affection? But it will be said that although kings and princes cannot make laws, but with the consent of the people, they may dispense with any positive law, by reason that a long time ago they used to, and prescribed so to do: for long custom makes a law.

To this it may be answered that evil customs (be they never so old) are not to be suffered, but to be utterly abolished: and none may prescribe to do evil, whether king or subject. If the laws appoint you to the term of thirty or forty years to claim a sure and perfect interest in what you enjoy, yet if you know that either yourself or those by whom you claim came wrongfully by it, you are not in deed a perfect owner of it, but are bound to restore it. Although the laws of man do excuse and defend you from outward trouble and punishment, yet they do not quiet the conscience, but when your conscience remembers that you enjoy is not yours, it will convict you that you have done wrong: it will accuse you before the judgment of God, and condemn you. And if princes and governors would show themselves to be half as wise as they would have men take them to be, and by the example of others learn what mischief might happen to themselves, they would not (if they might) claim, much less execute any such absolute authority. No, neither would their counselors (if they loved them) maintain them in it: nor would the subjects suffer their prince to do what he lusted for.

For the one purchases for themselves a perpetual

uncertainty of life and goods: and the other procures the hatred of all, although it be colored and dissembled for a season, yet it does not at length burst out, and works the revenge with extremity....

He is a good citizen that does not do evil (so said a noble wise man) but he is better who does not allow others to hurt or do injustice to the innocent. For the blood of the innocent shall be demanded not only from those that shed blood, but also of those that make or consent to wicked laws, to condemn the innocent, or suffer their head to kill them contrary to just laws, or to spoil then of what they justly enjoy be the order of law.

Now kings, princes, and governors of commonwealths have not, nor can justly claim, an absolute authority, but the end of their authority is the maintenance of justice, to defend the innocent, and to punish evil. And that so many evil and mischiefs may follow, where such absolute and, indeed, tyrannical power is usurped: let us pray that they may know their duty, and discharge themselves to God and to the world, or else that those which have the authority to reform them, may know and do their duty, that the people finding and acknowledging the benefit of good rulers, may thank God for them, and everyone labors to do their duty: and that saying–the head is not spared, but evil sin is punished–they may be more willing to abstain from tyranny and other evil doings, and do their duties, and all glorify God.

21

Chapter III. Whether Kings, Princes and other Governors are subject to God's laws, and the positive laws of their country.

One who observes the proceedings of princes and governors in these days will note how ambitious they are to usurp the dominions of others, and how negligent they are to see their own well governed, might think that wither there is no God, or that he has no care for the things of this world: or they think themselves exempt from God's laws and power. But the wonderful overthrow of their devices (when they think themselves most sure and certain) is so manifest, that it is not possible to deny that there is a God, and that he cares for the things of this world. And His word is so plain that none can contradict that they are to be subject and obedient to God's laws and word. For the whole Decalogue and every part thereof is written as well to kings, princes, and other public persons, as it is to private persons. A king may no more commit idolatry than a private man: he may not take the name of God in vain, he may not break the Sabbath, no more than any private man. It is not lawful for him to disobey his parents, to kill any person contrary to God's laws, to be a whoremonger, to steal, to lie and bear false witness, to desire and covet any man's house, wife, servant, maid, ox, ass, or anything that belongs to another, more than any other private man. No, he is bound and charged under great pains to keep them more than any other, because he is both a private man in respect of his own person, and a public figure in respect to his office, which may appear in a great many places which I will recite. The Holy Ghost said by the mouth of a king and a prophet: "And now you kings understand, and be learned you that judge the earth. Serve the Lord in fear, and rejoice with trembling. Kiss the Son (that is, receive with honor), lest the Lord become angry, and you lose the way, when His wrath shall in a moment be kindled." And in another place: "The Lord upon your right hand shall smite and break into pieces even kings in the day of His wrath." Isaiah, the prophet, also says: "The Lord shall come to judgment against the princes and elders of the people." Likewise, the Prophet Micah speaks to all princes and governors under the heads of the house of Jacob, and the leaders of the house of Israel: "Hear all you princes and governors. Should you not know what was lawful and right? But you hate the good, and love evil, you pluck off men's skin, and the flesh from their bones: you chop them into pieces, as it were in to a caldron, and as flesh in to a pot. Now the time shall come that when you call unto the Lord, He shall not hear you, but hide His face from you, because through your own imaginations you have dealt wickedly." And again he says: "O hear all you rulers and governors, you that abhor the thing that is lawful, and waste aside the thing that is straight: you that build up Zion with blood, your majesty and tyranny with wrong doing." So may Zion and Jerusalem be well expounded: "O you judges, you give sentence for gifts: O you priests, you teach for lucre: O you prophets, you prophesy for money: yet they will be taken as those that hold upon God and say, 'Is not the Lord among us? How can any misfortune happen to us?' But Zion (that is, your cities) for your sakes shall be plowed like a field: and Jerusalem (that is, your palaces) shall become a heap of stones, and the hill of the Temple (that is, your monasteries, friaries, and chantrys) shall become a high forest." The Holy Ghost also speaks by the mouth of King Solomon: "Hear, O you kings, and understand. O learn you that be judges of the ends of the earth. Give ear, you that rule the multitudes, and delight in many people. For the power given unto you is from the Lord, and the strength from the high heavens, who shall try your works, and search out your imaginations, how you being officers of His kingdom have not kept the law of righteousness, nor walked in His will. Horribly and soon He shall appear to you, for upon the highest among you, He will execute a most severe judgment. Mercy is granted unto the simple, but those that are in authority shall be punished. For God, who is Lord over all, shall not regard any man's person, neither shall He regard any man's greatness, for He cares alike for all. But the mighty shall have a sorer punishment. To you therefore (O princes) do I speak, that you may learn wisdom, and not offend....

Therefore, seeing no king or governor is exempted from the laws, hand, and power of God, but that he ought to fear and tremble at it, we may proceed to the other part of the question: that is, whether kings, princes, and other governors ought to be obedient to the positive laws of their country. To discuss this question, the right way and means is as in all other things, to resort to the fountains and roots, and not to depend on the rivers and branches. For if men should admit that the church of Rome were the catholic church, and the pope the head of it, and God's only vicar on earth, and not seek further how he comes by that authority: then no man could say that all his doings (were they never so wicked) should seem just: so if men should build upon the authority that kings and princes usurp over their subjects, and not seek from whence they have their authority, not whether that which they use, be just, there could be nothing produced to let their cruel tyranny. But as we see from whence all political power and authority comes, that is, from God: and why it was ordained, that is, to maintain justice: we ought (if we will judge rightly) by God's word examine and try this matter.

Saint Paul, treating the subject of who should be

obedient, and to whom obedience is due, says: "Let every soul be subject to the powers that rule, for there is no power but from God." There are some who would have this word, soul, taken to be man, not as he consists of soul and body both together, but only of the flesh: and by that word, soul, should be understood only as a worldly man, that is, a lay man or temporal man (as we term it) and not a spiritual man and a minister of the church. Where upon Antichrist, the bishop of Rome, seeking for subjects to be under his kingdom, has taken the clergy to be his subjects, along with everything that belongs to them: and he has made laws that they should be his subjects, obedient to him and not to the political power and authority, where he leaves subjects only the temporal....

But here it may be asked, who handed out this justice to kings and princes before that time, since it was only then committed to the bishop of Rome? We need not answer that at this time, for we do not seek presently to know who should be judge, but only the declare and prove that kings and princes ought, both by God's law, the law of nature, man's law, and good reason, to be obedient and subject to the positive laws of their country, and may not break them, and that they are not exempt from them, nor may dispense with them, unless the makers of the laws give them express authority to do so.

Who shall be the kings judge, you will hear later.

We Must Obey God Rather than Man

In the fourth chapter, John Ponet drew upon a comparison well-worn throughout English history: the great "Commonwealth" was very much like a single gigantic body. Just as the body is structured by bones and sinews, the English commonwealth required that the people keep themselves "in good order by obedience." To Ponet, however, recent events, ancient history, and Biblical teachings all proved in abundance that order and obedience need not be enforced by tyrannical rulers. When rulers became corrupted by their power, the commonwealth's great body became "racked and stretched too much," causing "great pain and deformity" on the society at large. Ponet attempted to steer a middle course between radical Protestants (notably the Anabaptists) and Catholics. Whereas the Anabaptists recognized no worldly powers, the Catholics sought a single (*papal*) ruler for all the peoples of the earth. For later theorists in the English tradition of whiggish republicanism—including John Adams—Ponet's arguments that subjects are ultimately responsible only to God and that kings, too, may be discarded and damned, proved both prophetic and timely.

Chapter IV. In what things, and how far subjects are bound to obey their princes and governors.

As the body of man is knit and kept together in due proportion by the sinews, so every commonwealth is kept and maintained in good order by obedience. But as the sinews are racked and stretched too much, or shrink together too much, it breeds great pain and deformity in a man's body: so if obedience is too much or too little in a commonwealth, it causes much evil and disorder. For too much makes the governors forget their vocation, and to usurp upon their subjects: too little breeds a licentious liberty, and makes the people to forget their duty. And so in both ways the commonwealth grows out of order, and at length comes to havoc and utter destruction.

Some will have too little obedience, as the Anabaptists. For when they heard of a Christian liberty, they would have had all political power taken away: and so in deed no obedience.

Others (as the English Papists) rack and stretch out obedience too much, and have no need of civil power obeyed in all things, and whatsoever it commands, without respect it ought and must be done. But both of them be in great error. For the Anabaptists mistake Christian liberty, thinking that men may live without sin, and forget the fall of man, whereby he was brought into such misery, that he is no more able to rule himself by himself, than one beast is able to rule another: and that therefore God ordained civil power (his minister) to rule him, and to call him back, whenever he should pass the limits of his duty, and would give an obedience back to him.

And the Papists neither consider the degrees of powers, nor over what things civil power has authority, nor how far subjects ought to obey their governors. And they do this not for a lack of knowledge, but from a spiritual malice, because it goes against their purpose, that the truth should be disclosed.

If any Christian prince should do about to redress the abuses of the Sacraments (brought in and devised by the Papists to maintain their kingdom) to

correct their abominable lies, their whoredom, buggery, drunkenness, pride, and other vices: then he is
another Ozias, another Osa, a heretic, a schismatic,
cursed from top to toe, with book, bell, and candle,
as black as a pot side: no obedience of the subjects
ought to be given unto him. But if he be content
to wink at their abominations, to run with them,
to dishonor God, to commit idolatry, to kill the
true ministers and counselors of Christ, to destroy
the poor innocents which abhor the Papist's wicked
vices, and be desirous that God's kingdom not be
promoted: then he is another Ezekiel, a Josiah, a
catholic prince, a dear son of the church, the protec-
tor of the church, the defender of the faith, the fos-
terer of the church, a counselor while he lives, after
his death a saint (yes, a saint devil) canonized with
Ora pro nobis: when Beelzebub dances at his dirge.

Such a one (they say) must be obeyed in all
things, not may speak against his proceedings, for
he that resists the power, resists the ordinance of
God, and he that resists, purchases for himself
damnation: as though to leave evil undone, and to
do good, were to resist the power. And here also
they wring this saying of Saint Peter (Servants obey
your masters, although they be froward and churl-
ish) to free subjects under a king: as if bondsmen
and freemen were alone, and king and bondsmen
had similar authority. So with violent wringing and
false application of God's life giving word, Caiphas
and Herod rode cheek by cheek, and arm in arm,

with both the swords and Cross before them. Friend to the one, friend to both: and he that is a heretic with Caiphas must be a traitor to Herod.

Thus they go about to blind men's eyes to confirm and increase their devilish kingdom. But popish prelate's practices are no warrant to discharge a Christian man's conscience. He must seek out what God would have him do, and not what the subtlety and violence of wicked men will force him to do. He may not rob Peter to clothe Paul, not take from God his due to give it unto civil power: neither may he make confusion of the powers, but yield unto everyone that is his due, not in obeying the inferior commandment, leave the commandment of the highest undone. "Yield unto Caesar, those things that be Caesar's," says Christ, "and unto God the things that be God's." Civil power is a power and ordinance of God, appointed to certain things, but no general minister over all things. God has not given it power over the one and best part of man, that is, the soul and conscience of man, but only over the other and the worst part of man, that is, the body, and those things that belong unto the temporal life of man.

And yet over that part with the appurtenances He has not only not given man the whole power, and stripped himself of all the authority, but also He has reserved to Himself the power thereof. For we read that when civil power (His minister) has been negligent in doing his duty, or winked at the evil life of the people, God has not held his hand, but has whipped and plagued such people, as he did the Sodomites, Gomorrians, and in diverse times, the Jews.

And in our days his hand is not short, but he has, and daily does, plague blasphemers, whoremongers, drunkards, murderers, thieves, traitors, tyrants, such as in man's sight no man would touch: some with incurable plagues of their body, some with loss of their children, some with the loss of their goods, and some with shameful deaths.

And to the contrary, when the worldly powers have violently, tyrannously, over sharply, and wrongfully oppressed and condemned innocents, God (to testify that He has also power of the body) has many times in all ages mightily and mirac- ulously delivered His people from the power of tyrants....

God is the highest power, the power of powers, from Him is derived all power. All people are His servants made to serve and glorify Him. All other powers are but His ministers, set to oversee that everyone behaves himself, as he should towards God, and to do those things, that he is justly com- manded to do by God.

Whatever God commands man to do, he ought not to consider the matter, but be straight to obey the commander. For we are sure, what He com- mands, is just and right: for from Him, that is, all together just and right, no injustice nor wrong can come....

But contrary in man's commandments, men ought to consider the matter, and not the man. For all men, whatever ministry or vocation they exercise, are but men, and so may err. We see councils against councils, parliaments against parliaments, commandments against commandments, this day one thing, tomorrow another. It is not the man's warrant that can discharge them, but it is the thing itself that must justify thee....

For the subjects ought not (against nature) to further their own destruction, but to seek their own salvation: not to maintain evil, but to suppress evil: for not only the doers, but also the consenters to evil, shall be punished, say both God's and man's laws. And men ought to have more respect to their country, than to their prince: to the commonwealth, than to any one person. For the country and commonwealth is a degree above the king. Next unto God, men ought to love their country, and the whole commonwealth before any member of it: as kings and princes (be they never so great) are but members: and commonwealths may withstand well enough and flourish, albeit there be no kings, but to the contrary, without a commonwealth there can be no king. Commonwealths and realms may live, when the head is cut off, and may put on a new head, that is , make them a new governor, then they see their old head seek too much his own will and not the wealth of the whole body, for which he was ordained. And by that justice and law, that lately has been executed in England (if it may be called justice and law) it should appear that the ministers of civil power do sometimes command that which the subjects ought not to do....

For although the king or queen of a realm have the Crown never justly, yet may they dispose of the Crown or realm, as it pleases them. They have the Crown to minister justice, but the realm being a body of free men and not of bondmen, he nor she can not give or sell them as slaves and bondsmen. No, they can not give or sell away the holds and forts (as Calais or Berwick, or such like) without the consent of the Commons: for it was purchased with their blood and money. Yea and thine own pope's laws (whereby you measure all things to be lawful or not lawful) say that if a king or governor of any realm do about to diminish the regalities and rights of his crown, he ought to be deposed....

Christ says: "He that does not take up his cross and follow me, is not mete for me". And again: "Blessed be those that suffer persecution for righteousness sake, for theirs is the kingdom of Heaven. Blessed are you when men shall curse you, and persecute you, and speak all evil against you, living for my sake: be glad and rejoice, for your reward is plentiful in Heaven. So did they persecute the Prophets that were before you". And the Apostle says: "All that live godly in Christ Jesus, shall suffer persecution". And so in a great number of places in Scripture.

But such persecution cannot be meant the injuries that private man does to private man: for God has ordained a means, that is, the magistrate to redress them. But by persecution is meant the injuries and tyranny that the magistrates and governors exercise over God's people. For they, not content to let a Christian man have justice in civil things against a papist, not an honest man against such a one as favors their proceedings, do themselves spoil the Christians and honesty of their goods: and not only spoil them, but by all manner of force, violence, and snares seek their life and blood, not only in their own country, but where then have no authority, because they will not obey their commandments, and follow their wicked proceedings.

God will have His tried by persecution, that the world may see, who love the chief power, more than the inferior powers: His commandments, more than man's fond proceedings: the soul, more than the flesh: the sure and everlasting inheritance of Heaven, more than the uncertain and temporal possessions of this world. Yea he has no other way to let the differences appear to men's eyes between His servants and parasite princes, than only by persecution....And yet God does not so severely require of his people, that they should offer themselves to the princes slaughterhouse, their necks to the halter, their heads to the block, their blood to make prince's pudding, their entrails to make tripes, their quarters to be boiled or roasted: but he has left them a special rule and commandment, whereby to guide themselves, that is, in all things to seek first the Kingdom of God. If he that is persecuted, feels in his conscience, that he may do God greater service and glorify by suffering than by fleeing, he ought rather to suffer a thousand deaths, that to flee one foot. But if his conscience witnesses with him that he may do God greater glory by fleeing that by tarrying, but is bound by the commandment to depart. "If they persecute you in one city," says Christ, "flee to another." And he did not only teach it, but did it himself, forsaking Jewry, and going into Galilee, when he heard John the Baptist was laid by the heels, because the time was not yet come, wherein he was appointed to glorify God. And because God would have a refuge place, and sanctuary for his, when such tyranny and persecution should be exercised, he would never suffer the power and ambitious tyrannies, to make one perfect monarchy of all, but when they had done their best to bring all together, and the string had been almost in the nick of the bow (as the proverb says) it had suddenly slipped, and not only destroyed the doer, but it has fallen into a great many shivers than it ever was before. Thus God dallies and plays with His puppets the prince of this world.

Since we be God's people and servants, and He our Lord and the highest power: and the princes

of the world be but his ministers and inferior powers, ordained to do good and not evil: we ought to
seek chiefly to do God's commandments before all
men, to please God rather than men. For the princes
(do they the worst they can) can but take from men
their goods and lives: but God can take from us
both goods and body, and cast both body and soul
into hell. And yet should not they be able to work
their will in this world, not execute their malice,
if men would behave themselves toward their Lord
and Master, God, as they ought. For as he can, so
would he soon dispatch the world of tyrants. But
because many be open enemies of God, and many
dissemblers of God, God sends and suffers evil governors (and will send worse) to plague the people for
their iniquity, and to try the faith of his Elect, from
whom not one hair of the head can be taken without God's will. And seeking always to do that which
is good, they should always eschew to do that which
is evil, and commit the end to God.

But admit there be a great number that have
drunk of the Whore of Babylon's cup, and think
that there is neither Heaven nor Hell, and that God's
word is but friars' matters: and that (like Sardana-
palus) they should seek to eat and drink, and serve
their lusts, and nothing else, were there no sure way
for them to do what they would, if they should obey
their princes in whatever they commanded.

The nature of wicked princes is much like to the
warthogs, which if they be suffered to have their

snouts in the ground, and be not forthwith let, will suddenly have in all the body: So they if they be obeyed in any evil thing (be it never so little) will be obeyed in all at length.... All the paper in England would not serve to record the mischief that might follow, then princes' evil commandments should be obeyed and fulfilled. But men that are wise, may by a little, consider the whole.

Seeing that God wills princes' commandments should not be obeyed in all things, but will have His rather suffer a thousand deaths, than do anything that is evil: and since also many evils and mischiefs may follow in this life, where wicked princes will may stand for laws, men ought, both for God's sake and commandment, abstain to obey such commandments, and cleave unto this maxim: We must obey God rather than man, for whose sake if we lose both goods and life, we ought to rejoice, that we be called to serve him, and not doubt, but as He is able to recompense it, so will He (according to His promise) reward it. And besides also they ought to consider, that princes be ordained for the wealth and benefit of the people, and not to their destruction: to maintain commonwealths, and not to subvert them: which rather that any man should consent unto, he ought (being a faithful man to his country) to abide all losses, both of body and goods. For next after God, men be born to love, honor, and maintain their country.

4

To Depose and Evil Governor, and Kill a Tyrant

In John Ponet's final remarks on political philosophy, the "Marian exile" Bishop of Winchester struck at the remaining roots of late medieval royalism. The *Short Treatise*'s fifth chapter dispels the feudal mythology that the king owned all the realm as his personal property. To Ponet, the *commonwealth* remained the prince's over-riding and proper interest. The good prince existed on a meager taxation and ruled wisely, purely for the good of his charges. Should worldly rulers exceed their natural and moral authorities, however, the sixth chapter argues that the people may go so far as executing kings.

No longer should the English labor under the false feudal idea that the king's body was a sacred instrument. Men—which is to say *all men*—were by nature corrupt and fallen. He and his contemporaries had only glance around them to see the results of evil, self-interested rulers. The Bishop concluded that "Kings, princes, and other governors, although they are the heads of a political body, yet they are not the whole body," and that sometimes even decapitation could be justified. Yet if the people refused to replace wicked leaders with new heads of state, they had only themselves to blame should God demolish their evil society.

Chapter V. Whether All The Subject's Goods Be The Kaisers and Kings Own, And That They May Lawfully Take Them As Their Own.

The Anabaptists wresting Scripture to serve their madness, among other foul errors, have this: that all things ought to be common, they imagine man to be of that purity that he was before the Fall, that is, clean without sin, or that (if he will) he may so be: and that as when there was no sin, all things were common, so they ought to be now.

But this mingling of the state of man before the Fall, and of him after the Fall deceives them much. For by the Fall, and ever after the Fall, this corruptible flesh of man is clogged with sin, and shall never be rid of sin, as long as it is in this corrupt world, but shall be always disposed and prone to do that which is evil. Therefore, as one means to be uncombered [unencumbered] of the heap of sin, God ordained that man should get his living by the sweat of the brow: and that he should be the more forced to labor, the distinction of things and property (mine, and yours) was (contrary to Plato's opinion) ordained, being apparent by these two laws: Thou shall not steal: Thou shall not covet your neighbor's wife, not his servant, nor his maid, nor his ox, nor his ass, nor anything that is his. Afterward, in deed, Scripture speaks of communion of things, not that they ought so to be (for so Scripture should be directly against Scripture) but that there was such charity among people, that of their own free will, they gave and sold all they had, to relieve the misery of their poor brethren: who for impotency, or for multitude of children, were not with their labor able to get sufficient to relieve their necessity. Nor of this so given might every man take as much as lusted for, but to everyone (according to his necessity) sufficient was distributed. So that it stood in the liberality of the giver, and not in the liberty of the taker.

But there are some in these days, not of the mean-

41

est or poorest sort, but of the chief and rich: that is, many wicked governors and rulers, who in this error excel the common Anabaptists. For the common Anabaptists do not only take other men's goods as common, but are content to let their own also be common, which smacks of some charity: for they themselves do not to others, but as they themselves are content to suffer.

But the evil governors and rulers will have all that their subjects have, common to themselves, but they themselves will depart with nothing, but where they ought not: no, not so much as pay for those things, that in words they pretend to buy of their subjects, not pay those poor men their wages, whom they force to labor and toil in their works. But the manner of coming thereby is so divers, that it makes the justness of their doings much suspect. For some do it under pretense to do the people good: some by crafty and subtle means, color their doings: and some of right (but without right) claim them for their own.

Of the first sort are those, that put great taxes and impositions on drink, for as much as the people with overmuch drinking become drunkards (and so sin against God) they would seem by making them pay as much or more to them as the drink is worth, they should force them the rather to abstain from too much drinking, and so from sin. But in this it may appear they seek not abstinence from sin, and the wealth of the people, but their own private profit....

The second sort be those that rob the people indeed, yet would not have their doings known. They walk in nets, and think no man sees them. And of this kind be those, that contrary to all laws (both of God and man) and contrary to their other, changing the coin that is ordained to run between man to man, turning the substance from gold to copper, from silver to worse than pewter, and advancing and diminishing the price at their pleasure....

The third sort of these evil princes are those that claim all their subjects' goods for their own, who allege for them this common saying: All things are the Kaiser's, all things be the king's, all things be the prince's. And as the devil brought forth Scripture to serve his purpose against Christ, so they abhorring all other parts of Scripture, that teach them their office or Christian duty, pike out only a piece that may maintain their tyranny...

But let us imagine an untruth, that all the subjects' goods were the princes', and that he might take them at his pleasure. Let us imagine, that the subjects were only carnal men without knowledge and fear of God. Yes, and let it be granted also, that they were spoiled of all their armor, and great garrisons set in every place to keep them in office, so that they had not wherewith to address their injuries, as nature would counsel them: were this a way to make the people labor, when others should take the bread out of their mouths? Would they desire to

43

increase the world with children, when they knew that they should be left in the worst estate, than unreasonable beasts? No surely, and that you may see by the work of nature in the people of the West Indies, now called New Spain: who knew of Christ nothing at all, and of God no more that nature taught them. The people of that country when the Catholic Spaniards came to them, were simple and plain men, and lived without great labor, the land was naturally so plentiful of all things, and continually the trees had ripe fruit on them. When the Spaniards had by flattery put in their foot, and little by little made themselves strong, building forts in various places, they to get the fold that was there, forced the people (that were not used to labor) to stand all the day in the hot sun gathering gold in the sand of the rivers. By this means a great number of them (not used to such pains) died, and a great number of them (seeing themselves brought from so quiet a life to such misery and slavery) of depression killed themselves. And many would not marry, because they would not have their children slaves to the Spaniards. The women when they felt themselves with child, would eat a certain herb to destroy the child in the womb. So that where at the coming of the Spaniards, there were believed to be in that country nine hundred thousand persons, there were in short time by this means so few left, as Peter Martyr (who was one of the Emperor Charles the

44

fifth's counsel there, and wrote this history to the Emperor) says, it was a shame for him to name.

This is the fruit, where princes take all their subjects things as their own. And where at length will it come, but that either they must be no kings, or else kings without people, which is all one. But you will say: where comes this common saying: all things be the kaiser's, all things be the king's? It cannot come from nothing. But with that already said, you see that every man may keep his own, and none may take it from him, so that it cannot be interpreted, that all things be the kaiser's or king's, as his own property, or that they may take them from their subjects at their pleasure, but thus it is to be expounded, that they ought to defend what every man has, that he may quietly enjoy his own, and to see that they be not robbed or spoiled thereof....The prince's watch ought to defend the poor man's house, his labor the subject's ease, his diligence the subject's pleasure, his trouble the subject's quietness. And as the sun never stood still but continually goes about the world, doing his office: with his heat refreshing and comforting all natural things in the world: so ought a good prince to be continually occupied in his ministry, not seeking his own profit, but the wealth of those that are committed to his charge....

Chapter VI. Whether It Be Lawful To Depose An Evil Governor, And Kill A Tyrant.

As there is no better nor happier commonwealth nor no greater blessing of God, than where one rules, if he is a good, just, and godly man: so there is no worse nor none more miserable, nor greater plague of God, than where one rules, that is evil, unjust and ungodly. A good man knowing that he or those by whom he claims was to such office called for his virtue, to see the whole state well governed, and the people defended from injuries: neglecting utterly his own pleasure and profit, and bestows all his study and labor to see his office well discharged. And as a good physician earnestly seeks the health of his patient and a shipmaster the wealth and safeguard of those he has in his ship, so does a good governor seek the wealth of those he rules. And therefore the people feeling the benefit coming by good governors, used in times past to call such good governors, fathers: and gave them no less honor than children owe to their parents. An evil person coming to the government of any state, either by usurpation, or by election or by succession, utterly neglecting the cause why kings, princes, and other governors in commonwealths be made (that is, the wealth of the people) seeks only or chiefly his own profit and pleasure. And as a sow coming into a fair garden, roots up all the fair

and sweet flowers and wholesome simples, leaving
nothing behind, but her own filthy dirt: so does an
evil governor subvert the laws and orders, or makes
them to be wrenched or racked to serve his affec-
tions, that they can no longer do their office. He
spoils the people of their goods, either by open violence, making his ministers to take it from them
without payment therefore, or promising and never
paying: or craftily under the mane of loans, benev-
olences, contributions, and such gay painted words,
or forbear he gets out of their possession that they
have, and never restores it. And when he has it, con-
sumes it, not to the benefit and profit of the commonwealth, but on whores, whoremongers, dice
games, cards, bankletting, unjust wars, and such
evils and mischiefs, wherein he delights. He spoils
and takes away from them their armor and harness,
that they shall not be able to use any force to defend
their right. And not content to have brought them
in to such misery (to be sure of his state) seeks and
takes all occasions to dispatch them of their lives. If
a man keeps his house, and nothing in metal, than
shall it be said that he frets at the state. If he comes
abroad and speaks to any other, further with it is
taken for a just conspiracy. If he says nothing, and
shows a merry countenance, it is a token, that he
despises the government. If he look sorrowful, than
he laments the state of his country, how many so
ever be for any cause committed to prison, are not
only asked, but are racked also to show whether he

is privy of their doings. If he departs, because he would live quietly, then he is proclaimed an open enemy. To be short, there is no doing, no gesture, no behavior, no place can preserve or defend innocence against such a governor's cruelty: but as a hunter makes wild beasts his pray, and uses toils, nets, snares, traps, dogs, ferrets, mining and digging the ground, guns, bows, spears, and all other instruments, engines, subtle devises and means, whereby he may come by his prey: so does a wicked governor make the people his game and prey, and uses all kinds of subtleties, deceits, crafts, policies, force, violence, cruelty, and such devilish ways, to spoil and destroy the people, that be committed to his charge. And when he is not able without most manifest cruelty to do by himself that which he desires, then fain unjust causes to cast them into prison, where like as the bearwards muzzle the bears, and tie them to the stakes, while they are baited and killed by mastiffs and curies, so he keeps them in chains, while the bishops and his other tormentors and heretical inquisitors do tear and devour them. Finally, he says and denies, he promises and breaks promises, he swears and forswears, and no other passes on God nor the devil (as the common saying is) so he may bring to pass that which he desires. Such an evil governor men properly call a tyrant.

Now for as much as there is no express positive law for punishment of a tyrant among Christian men, the question is, whether it is lawful to kill such

a monster and cruel beast covered with the shape of
a man.

And first for the better and more plain prose of
this matter, the manifold and continual examples
that have been from time to time of the deposing of
kings, and killing of tyrants, do most certainly confirm it to be most true, just and constant to God's
judgment. The history of kings in the Old Testa-
ment is full of it....

But here you see the body of every state may
(if it will) yea and ought to redress and correct the
vices and heads of their governors. And for as much
as you have already seen, whereof political power
and government grows, and the end where unto
it was ordained: and seeing it is before manifestly
and sufficiently proved, that kings and princes have
not an absolute power over their subjects: that they
are and ought to be subject to the law of God, and
the wholesome positive laws of their country: and
that they may not lawfully take or use their subjects'
goods at their pleasure: the reasons, arguments, and
law that serve for the deposing and displacing of an
evil governor, will do as much for the proof, that it
is lawful to kill a tyrant, if they may be indifferently
heard. As God has ordained magistrates to hear and
determine private men's matters, and to punish their
vices: so also will he, that the magistrate's doings be
called into account and reckoning, and their vices
corrected and punished by the body of the whole
congregation or commonwealth....

For in some places and countries they have more and greater authority, in some places less. And in some the people have not given this authority to any other, but retain and exercise it themselves. And is any man so unreasonable to deny, that the whole may do as much as they have permitted one member to do? Or those that have appointed an office upon trust, have not authority upon just occasion (as the abuse of it) to take away that they gave? All laws do agree, that men may revoke their proxies and letters of Attorney, when it pleased them: much more when they see their proctors and attorneys abuse it....

For it is no private law to a few or certain people, but common to all: not written in books, but grafted in the hearts of men: not made by man, but ordained of God: which we have not learned, received or read, but have taken, sucked, and drown it out of nature: where unto we are not taught, but made: not instructed, but seasoned: and (as St. Paul says) man's conscience bearing witness of it.

This law testifies to every man's conscience, that it is natural to cut away an incurable member, which (being suffered) would destroy the whole body.

Kings, princes, and other governors, although they are the heads of a political body, yet they are not the whole body. And though they be the chief members, yet they are but members: no other are the people ordained for them, but they are ordained for the people....

Good kings, governors, and states in time past took it to be the greatest honor that could be, not to take cities and realms to their own use (when they were called to aid and relieve the oppressed) as princes do now a days: but to rescue and deliver the people and countries from the tyranny of the governors, and to restore them to their liberties....

If a prince robs and spoils his subjects, it is theft, and as a thief ought to be punished. If he kills and murders them contrary or without the laws of his country, it is murder, and a murderer he ought to be punished. If he commits adultery, he is an adulterer and ought to be punished with the same pains that others be. If he violently ravish men's wives, daughters, or maidens, the laws that are made against ravishers, ought to be executed on him. If he goes about to betray his country, and to bring the people under a foreign power: he is a traitor, and as a traitor he ought to suffer. And those that be judges in commonwealths, ought (upon complaint) to summon and cite them to answer to their crimes, and so to proceed, as they do with others....

And where this justice is not executed, but the prince and the people play together, and one winks and bears with the other's faults, there cannot be, but a most corrupt, ungodly, and vicious state, which although it prosper for a season, yet no doubt at length they may be sure, that unto them shall come that came to Sodom, Gomorrah, Jerusalem, and such other, that were utterly destroyed.

And on the other side, where the nobility and people look diligently and earnestly upon their authorities, and do see the same executed on their heads and governors, making them to yield account of their doings: then without fail will the princes and governors be as diligent to see the people do their duty. And so shall the commonwealth be godly, and prosper, and God shall be glorified in all. But you will say, that if the nobility, and those that be called to common Councils, and should be the defenders of the people, will not or dare not execute their authority: what is then to be done? The people be not so destitute of remedy, but God has provided another means, that is, to complain to some minister of the word of God, to whom the keys be given to excommunicate not only common people for all notorious and open evils: but also kaisers, kings, princes, and all other governors, when they spoil, rob, undo and kill their subjects without justice and good laws....

5

O, Miserable England

In the conclusion Ponet exhorted (or rather warned) his
countrymen in England to rise in their God-given
strength to hurl back the Catholic usurpers. Our author
looks to the cosmos for signs of doom, having already
found abundant horrors on Earth. He invokes history as
well as mysticism, recalling for his audience the destruction brought to England with William the Conqueror.
Englishmen indeed had only to consult their own gur-
gling stomachs to discover how dire were their times.
"When were ever things so dear in England," he asks,
"as in this time of the popish Mass and other idolatries
restored?" Although he does not explicitly call for the
English to execute Queen Mary in the streets, he

earnestly warns them that God's unrelenting fury awaits those societies that failed to chastise corrupted rulers. Ponet died shortly after publishing this book, still exiled in Strasbourg. His powerful arguments long out-lived him, however, and a century later the English finally took it upon themselves to execute their king. This time, yet another Catholic family had seized the throne and violated the commonwealth's good order. Charles I paid for his tyranny with his head, and after a brief interlude in republican tyranny, the crown returned as a much-weakened institution. A century after that, John Adams declared Ponet's ideas among the earliest and most important precursors to American republican thought.

An Exhortation, Or Rather, A Warning, To The Lords And Commoners Of England.

There was never great misery, destruction, plague, or visitation of God, that came on any nation, city, or country, which as they be indeed, so may they justly be called wounds, but be sent of God for sin, and be not suddenly laid on the people, but are before prophesied and declared by the prophets and ministers of God's word, or by some revelations, wonders, monsters in the earth, or tokens and signs in the elements.

For God as He is most just, and will not fail to punish sin, so is He most merciful, and wills not the death of sinners, but rather that they should turn to him and live.

And therefore beforehand gives them warning what shall follow, it in time they repent not, as by the histories of all ages it does appear. And none of these admonitions have you lacked, countrymen.

For the preachers and ministers of God's word, in the time of the godly Josiah, King Edward the Sixth preached and prophesied unto you, what miseries and plagues should certainly come to you....

But then you passed nothing on it...you laughed and jested at your preachers' words, nothing regarding the threats of God, but containing them, yes increasing in your wickedness, and now at length murdering most cruelly the minister of God.

And seeing words of warning took no place with you, God for His loving mercy has warned you also by monstrous marvels on the earth, and horrible wonders in the elements, to put you beside all manner of excuses. What wonderful monsters have there now lately been born in England?...

The horrible comet and blazing star that was seen this year greater in England than elsewhere, what else does it signify, but the great displeasure of God? And therefore famine, pestilence, wars, sedition, death of princes, invasion of foreign nations, destruction of some or many cities and countries, and the alteration and changing of the state and government? For if it be lawful for man to divine of God's wonderful works, and by the like things past, conjecture those that be to come: why should we not affirm, that these plagues will follow? Before the great wars made by Xerxes against the Greeks, and the overthrowing of the whole state of Greece, there was a blazing star seen of the shape of a horn, and an eclipse of the sun....

In the year 1061, before the invasion of William the Conqueror into England, and the conquest of the same, and in which Harold, King of England with twenty thousand true Englishmen in the defense of their country against a tyrant were slain: there was seen a wonderful comet, which every man thought (as indeed it followed) to be much mischief and the alteration of the state, as hereafter you shall hear. A little before the great wars in Normandy (whereof you have heard before) there was seen in Normandy a great comet, and two full moons at one time shining, the one in the East, the other in the West....

In what nation under the scope of Heaven, has God showed greater tokens of his Savior, and it so little set by, as in England? What contempt of Him, His word and ministers has there been? What dissimulation with God? What hypocrisy? What swearing and foreswearing? What treason to their country? What disobedience to the governors in good, godly, and necessary things? What ready obedience to their rulers in wicked and evil things? What unnatural relations used between the father and daughter, brother and sister? What abominable whoredom suffered unpunished? Yea in many and the chiefest places the greatest whoremongers, the most imprudent ribalds, the worst bribers, and the lewdest persons made Justices of the Peace, and correctors of vice? What railing and reviling of the worthy pure preachers of God's Gospel for only rebuking of vice? What horrible murders secret and open, not only of private persons, but also of the most honorable peers and reverend ministers of God? What butchering and burning of true English Christians, young and old, whole and lame, seeing and blind, man , woman, and child, without respect of age, sex or estate? What pillaging and pulling, taking and snatching, stealing and robbing, not only among the mean sort, but among the greatest? Where is so great hatred and malice, so little love and charity, as in England? I should never make an end, if I should tell but that I have myself seen and known, much less if I should declare all that other credible persons of their own knowledge report to be most certain and true.

But to return to the matter. Look well England, look well, whether the comet past, and eclipses to come, touch them? Are you not all ready plagued with famine? Yes, and with such a famine, as you

57

never before heard of....When were ever things so dear in England, as in this time of the popish Mass and other idolatries restored? Who ever heard or read before, that a pound of beef was at four pounds. A sheep twenty shillings. A pound of candles at four pounds. A pound of butter at four shillings. A pound of cheese at four pounds, two eggs a penny, a quart of wheat, sixty-three shillings. A quart of malt at fifty shillings, or above: the people driven of hunger to grind acorns for bread meal, and to drink water instead of ale? And what? Shall this famine away, before his walking mate and fellow (pestilence) come? No surely, without your earnest speedy repentance, and God's exceeding miraculous mercy, it is not possible: for hitherto the one went never before, but the other come either arm in arm, or else quickly after.

But it shall almost come too late for common people, for they are so hanged up by twenty and forty in a plump (and a great number of them, because they confessed and professed, that they should be saved by the only merits of Christ's passion) that the pestilence shall have little matter among the mean sort to be occupied on: but therefor must be the more occupied with the great.

And have you (England) had no sedition and inward grudge? Yes, so much that the heads and governors do not peep out of their privy chambers: not one neighbor seen to talk with another, for fear to be noted and accused of conspiracy. Yea and that

(that is worst of all, and to be lamented of all Englishmen) there is inward grudge, and secret malice
between the members, that is, the nobility and commoners.

The one hates and condemns the other, which is
the work of the devil, and his ministers the popish
prelates and priests. They cast water into the coals,
to make the fire greater: for they know, unless such
division and dissension be fostered and nourished,
their kingdom would soon lie in the dirt. This is
the practice of such as mind the conquest or utter
destruction of any people, to maintain and prick
forward dissension, division, and discord among the
people. For Christ's words are true, who says that
every kingdom divided against itself shall be deso-
late, and every city or house divided against itself,
shall not continue….

Who that fears your wrath, O Lord, will not
amend his life, and call to you for mercy? What
naughty nobility were that, that would oppress the
commoners, and afterward be used and oppressed
themselves, by strangers, as their predecessors have
been before time? What devilish commoners might
that be called that would repine or rebel against
the nobility and gentlemen, and then to be overrun
themselves: with priests and foreigners, and to be
pined with such misery, as you hear that our ances-
tors were: and all because the gentlemen and commoners agreed not among themselves? Who is a
natural Englishman, that will not in time foresee

and consider the misery toward his country and himself, and by all means seek to let it? Who is it, that can hope for quietness, peace, health, plenty, and such like gifts of God, without God's favor and mercy? And how is it possible that God should use mercy with them, that bears inward hatred and grudge one to another, and will use no mercy with others? If you forgive other men their offenses that they commit against you (says Christ) your Heavenly Father will forgive the offenses that you have committed against him. But if you do not forgive other men their faults, neither will your Father forgive you your faults. No while you say the Lord's Prayer, and be full of rancor, malice, hatred, and envy toward you neighbor, you condemn yourselves, and desire God's plagues and vengeance to fall on yourselves: for you mean vengeance to your neighbors, and wish all evil to fall on them. And so it does fall on you....

Remember, remember (good countrymen, and true English hearts) the misery that followed in our poor country upon the conquest made by the ambitious William, Duke of Normandy: upon how small a title he entered, and how tyrannously he used himself. His only color was a bequest or promise made to him by King Edward, brother to Cauntas and Harold, kings of England, when he was a banished man in Normandy, if he should die without issue, as he did. At his first entry, he had a great battle with the new chosen king of England, and slew him and twenty thousand of our countrymen, which put such a fear in all men, the nobility, the clergy, the Londoners, and the commoners, that it made them sue for peace, and to give pledges for their fidelity, whom he sent into Normandy....

He spoiled the nobility of their goods and possessions, made them slaves, and his own slaves lords: and upon the commoners he put immense taxes and impositions. He took from the people their weapons and harness, and made a law that no man should come out of his house after [eight o'clock]....He executed many wonderful cruel things, and specially on the nobility, and such as he saw to be stout men: some he caused to be murdered, some their nostrils to be slit, and their hands cut off. Happy was he that could fly out of the realm: he so spoiled Yorkshire, and Durham, and all the north ports, that ten years together it lay waste and uninhabited. He could in no wise abide the English nobility, but utterly destroyed them. And all this he did by the law of the devil, which they call the law of arms. The good laws and customs of England he clean took away, and made his own lusts his laws, and put them in his own Norman tongue, that his friends might always have the interpretation of them, and that he might catch the poor Englishmen, when it pleased him: and would have the laws to be pleaded and all things to be done in French. And he was not taken to be the Norman's friend, nor a gentleman, that could not speak French. And thereof

comes the old proverb : Jack would be a gentleman, but he cannot French. He removed the English bishops, and placed Normans by the aide of the
bishop of Rome. He pulled down towns, villages,
and houses, and put out the poor people to make
him sporting places, pricey pleasures, forts, pikes,
and chases. O miserable England, that once thus
was by a tyrant and outward enemies plagued. but
how much more miserable shall you be by the wars
that are most certain to come shortly to be. God be
merciful unto thee. But I think I hear your papists,
bishops, priests, friars, and such like antichristian
monsters say, that these plagues which have fallen
and shall come to England (for they know they cannot be avoided, no they are occasioned and helped
forward by them) have grown for things done in
King Henry and King Edward's time, for that their
abomination was disclosed, their burrows and dens
dug up, their monasteries thrown down, and the
lands divided and sold to the laity. Ah hypocrites,
ah subtle wolves, ah viperous generation. When the
fox preaches, beware you geese. Where in Scripture
do they find, that any such belly gods as they are,
should be maintained? No, Scripture would have
such merchants whipped out of the church, such
burrows and cellars of men's souls. Wo be unto
you hypocrites (says Christ) for you swallow up the
houses of the poor and miserable, that is, that which
should be converted to the relief of the poor and
needy: and that under pretense of long prayers. Wo

be unto you (you masking hounds) which go from place to place, by sea and by land, to make a novice of your own order, and when you have him, you make him the child of hellfire twofold more than yourselves. I know you not (says Christ) away from me, you workers of iniquity. It is only their god, the belly, that they seek to serve, they pass on the God in Heaven, nor the devil in hell, so they may have wherewith to maintain themselves on earth, in their whoredom, buggery, pride, and all abomination. And this I say, is not feigned or imagined, but evident in all men's eyes that will not be willfully blind....

But you will say: what shall we do to avoid the calamity and misery that is both present and toward? Would to God you did ask it from the bottom of your heart. But I fear you do dissemble and speak it with your lips only, as you were wont....All these plagues that before you have heard rehearsed, famine, pestilence, sedition, wars, destruction of countries, captivity of people, and alterations of states, are the instruments of God sent and powered on the people for their sins, that they should be sorry and repent them of their former wicked life, call to God for mercy, and lead a new life in holiness and righteousness all the days of their life: which if you will earnestly do, no doubt but as God is merciful, so will He use mercy towards you. For God that never deceived any, but abhors all practices, all deceit, and all practicers (the workers of deceit) promised it by the mouth of His prophet Ezekiel. If (He says) the ungodly will turn away from all his sins that he has done, and will keep all my commandments, and of the thing that is just and right, doubtless he shall live and not die. For all the sins that he did before, shall not be thought upon anymore: but in his righteousness that he has done, he shall live. For I have no pleasure in the death of a sinner (says God) but that he should repent him of his wicked life and live &etc. It follows in the prophet thus: wherefore repent and return from your wickedness, and your wickedness shall not be your destruction. Cast from you all your ungodliness, make you a new heart and a new spirit: wherefore will you die, O you house of Israel (that is, all such as trust to be saved by Christ) seeing I have no pleasure in the death of him that dies, say the Lord God. Turn therefore, and you shall live.

...If you will in time earnestly repent you of your sins, leave your idolatry, and honor and worship God truly, as you were taught in blessed King Edward's time, abhor the fantasies and foolish traditions of men, and cleave to the sincere word of God, and be desirous for the knowledge of it: leave your blasphemy and vain swearing and horrible forswearing and perjury, no longer hate your country, but be true and faithful to it, and by all godly means seek the wealth and safety of it: if you will obey God's commandments before your governors, and your governors in that [which] is godly, honest, and just, and nothing else: If you will leave your bawdry, whoredom, and improper relations, and drive out of all places whores, whoremongers, and whorehouses, and all such as favor and maintain them: If you will abstain from cruel murdering of the saints of God and innocents, and rather yourselves to be content to suffer all martyrdom, then you will embrew your fingers in their blood, or consent to it: If you will leave oppressing of your neighbors, your subtlety, craft, and deceit, and yourselves leave to love greediness, and inordinate desire of the trash of this world: If you leave your inward hate, greed, grudge and malice one to another, if the nobility will love and cherish the commonality, and the commoners honor and love the nobility: If one will show himself a brother and neighbor indeed to another: then no doubt if you do these things from the bottom of your heart, that the mouth and heart agree together, your sayings and doings be all one: then shall you perceive, that God will be easily entreated to turn. Then may you boldly ask of God in Christ's name, and your desires shall be heard and granted....Then will He send you His benediction for malediction, plenty for famine, health for pestilence, peace for wars, quietness for trouble, for cruel tyranny, a godly and just government: for sedition, such force and power, that you being a few, shall be able to withstand all the tyrannies of the world, and enemies of God and our country, and utterly confound them and destroy them. You shall avoid the eternal pains of hell prepared for sinners: and at length you shall be sure also to make a change from your earthly country to the Heavenly Paradise: from variable England, to the constant Jerusalem: from the company of men, to the fellowship of angels: from mutable and frowning countenances of worldly powers, to the unchangeable and most comfortable sight of the King of all Kings, our most merciful Eternal Heavenly Father. To whom with the Son and the Holy Ghost, be all honor, praise, and glory, now and forever. Amen.

Libertarianism.org

Liberty. It's a simple idea and the linchpin of a complex system of values and practices: justice, prosperity, responsibility, toleration, cooperation, and peace. Many people believe that liberty is the core political value of modern civilization itself, the one that gives substance and form to all the other values of social life. They're called libertarians.

Libertarianism.org is the Cato Institute's treasury of resources about the theory and history of liberty. The book you're holding is a small part of what Libertarianism.org has to offer. In addition to hosting classic texts by historical libertarian figures and original articles from modern-day thinkers, Libertarianism.org publishes podcasts, videos, online introductory courses, and books on a variety of topics within the libertarian tradition.